CONTENTS

HOORAY FOR HORSES!

The earliest relatives of today's horses lived on Earth around 55 million years ago. Some were no larger than a small dog! They all ran wild. However, humans changed the course of horse history. Humans found uses for horses as farm animals that could pull carts and wagons. People also rode horses to get from place to place. Horses pulled carriages and sleighs before—and even after—cars were invented.

More than 200 different horse **breeds** exist today. Very few wild horses are left. Most horses today are **domesticated**. That means they have **adapted** to being around people over the years. They are working animals. In this book, you'll learn how to draw eight different horses.

The first horses to be domesticated lived in present-day southern Russia and Kazakhstan around 3500 BCE. They were then sent along trade routes. They were used to pull carts, wagons, and chariots. The first horse we'll draw is the Arabian horse, which has been used for more than 4,000 years.

Gather your drawing materials!

You'll need a pencil, pencil sharpener, eraser, and paper. You might want to make your drawings in a sketch pad.

MEET THE ARABIAN HORSE

The Arabian horse's history may date back to 2000 BCE. That makes it one of the oldest horse breeds in the world. It appears in art from ancient Egypt and rock carvings found in Saudi Arabia.

The Arabian horse was raised in the deserts of the Middle East and North Africa by **nomadic** people called Bedouins. These people relied on their horses for survival. Because Arabian horses were raised by people who were on the move, they **developed** the ability to walk for a long time without stopping. During the seventh century CE, the Arabian was introduced to other countries when the religion of Islam began to spread across North Africa and into Spain. These horses were often used in war and trade.

Because of their close contact with humans, Arabian horses are usually comfortable with people. They are also very smart.

1

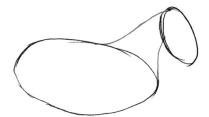

Begin drawing the body of the Arabian by making an oval as shown.

2

For the head, draw a smaller oval at the upper right of the larger one. Notice how much smaller it is and where it is placed on the page.

3

Connect the ovals with two curved lines to draw the neck.

4

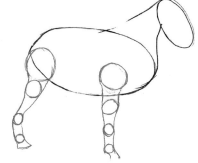

Draw eight circles—four for one front leg and four for one back leg. The circles get smaller as you go down the body. Join each set of circles with two curved lines, and draw hooves.

5

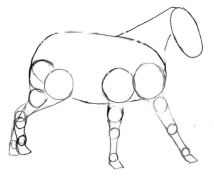

Then, draw the same shapes for the other two legs by drawing circles and connecting them with lines as shown.

6

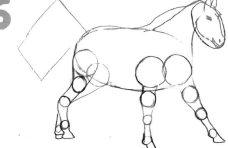

It's time to add some detail to the head. Draw the lower jaw, an eye, a nostril, the mouth, and the ears. Then, make the basic shapes of the tail and mane as shown.

7

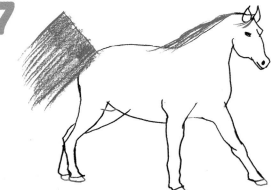

You can now erase any extra lines. Shade in the tail and the mane by holding the pencil with your index finger and using the side of the pencil point at a slant. Make big, wide strokes. Your Arabian horse looks awesome!

MEET THE SHIRE HORSE

The shire horse is one of the largest horse breeds on Earth. It gets its name from its main breeding areas: the English counties of Lincolnshire, Leicestershire, Staffordshire, and Derbyshire. In the Middle Ages, shires were used as warhorses, but today they are most often used to pull carts and carriages.

The shire horse is a draft horse, which is a type of horse that pulls loads such as wagons and plows. Draft horses are bigger and stronger than most other horses. A shire horse weighs about 1,800 pounds (816.5 kg). Horses are measured in "hands," or units of 4 inches (10.2 cm) each. The shire horse grows to about 17 hands tall!

When people take carriage rides in cities such as New York City, they may be pulled by a shire horse.

1

Begin drawing the body of the shire horse by making an oval as shown.

2

Above and to the right of the large oval, draw a smaller oval for the head.

3

Connect the ovals with two curved lines to make the neck.

4

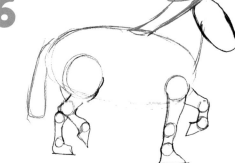

Next, form two of the legs by first drawing three circles for each leg. Draw two lines to join the circles. Then, add shapes for the hooves.

5

Now, draw the other legs and hooves. First, draw circles, and then add the lines to connect them.

6

Look to the illustration as you draw the shapes of the tail and mane.

7

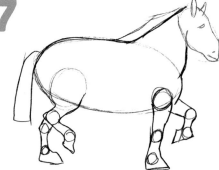

Draw the lower jaw, an eye, a nostril, the mouth, and both ears. Add a line to the front raised hoof as shown.

8

You can now erase any extra lines. Use the side of the pencil at a slant to shade in the tail, mane, and hooves. Time to share your shire horse!

MEET THE MUSTANG

The Spanish brought horses to the Americas in the 16th century. These horses are known as mustangs. Eventually, herds of mustangs could be found running wild in North America. They roamed in large groups across the Great Plains. They aren't true wild horses, though. Domesticated horses that turn wild, such as the mustangs of North America, are called feral horses.

Ranchers and cowboys called these wild horses broncos. They captured mustangs and trained them. Mustangs were **crossbred** with other horses to make strong workhorses for pulling wagons and **stagecoaches**. Wild mustangs were hunted for their meat in the 20th century, and their populations decreased greatly. Some still live on the plains of the United States.

In 1971, Congress passed a law that protects wild mustangs from hunters. Feral mustang herds are found in states such as Montana, Wyoming, and the Dakotas.

1

Begin drawing the body of the mustang by making an oval as shown.

2

Above and to the left of the first oval, draw a smaller oval for the mustang's head.

3

Connect the ovals with two curved lines to draw the neck.

4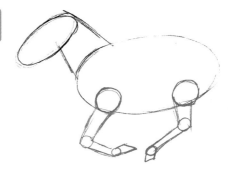

Draw three circles for each leg in the front and back as shown. The circles should be different sizes. Join them with lines, and then add hooves.

5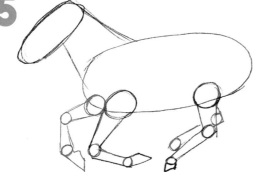

Now, follow those same steps for the other legs. Draw circles, and then connect them with lines. Remember to add the front hoof as shown.

6

Make the lower jaw, an eye, a nostril, a mouth, and both ears. Add the shape for the other back hoof. Then, add the curved shapes of the tail, neck, and mane as shown.

7

You can now erase any extra lines. Use the side of the pencil point to shade in the tail and the mane. That's a mighty mustang!

MEET THE PRZEWALSKI'S HORSE

Przewalski's horses are the only true wild horses left on Earth. They are native to Mongolia, a country in Asia. In 1881, a Russian army officer named Nikolai Przewalski discovered and described wild horses he found in Mongolia. The horse was named after him. It's also called the Asiatic wild horse or Mongolian wild horse.

Przewalski's horses are generally smaller than domesticated horses. They have a stocky body, a large head, and short legs. This species, or kind, of horse is in danger of dying out because of the actions of humans. **Conservation** efforts and zoos have helped keep this kind of horse alive.

In 1992, scientists reintroduced 16 Przewalski's horses back into their natural habitat in Mongolia. Today, there are hundreds of them in the wild.

1

Begin by drawing a beanlike shape for the horse's body.

2

Next, draw a smaller oval for the head. Notice where it's placed on the page compared to the first shape.

3

To draw the neck, connect the shapes with two curved lines.

4

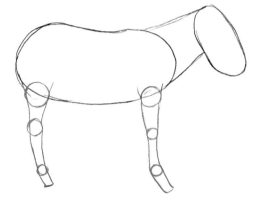

To add one front and one back leg, draw three circles for each leg. Draw two sets of curved lines as shown to join each set of circles. Connect these lines at the bottom with straight lines.

5

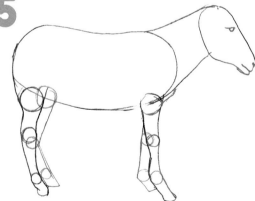

Follow the same directions as in Step 4 for the other legs by drawing circles and connecting them. Then you can draw the jaw, ear, eye, nostril, and mouth.

6

Now, erase any extra lines on your drawing. Make the basic shapes of the tail and mane. Notice how this horse's mane is shorter than that of other horses. Using the side of your pencil instead of the point, shade in the mane and tail. Your Przewalski's horse is perfect!

MEET THE QUARTER HORSE

The quarter horse was a popular horse in the American colonies. The quarter horse is part English Thoroughbred and part Spanish. In the early 1600s, horses that had been brought from England were bred with the horses that had been brought to North America in the 1500s by the Spaniards. The result was the quarter horse.

The quarter horse got its name because it could win races that were a quarter of a mile (0.4 km) long. American **colonists** in Rhode Island and Virginia raced quarter horses often. In addition to racing, quarter horses were used on cattle ranches. The quarter horse is one of the most popular horses in the world today.

Cowboys in the Old West depended on these quick and **agile** horses to control their herds of cattle.

1

Begin by drawing a beanlike shape for the quarter horse's body.

2

Next, draw a small oval for the head a little above and to the right of the first shape as shown.

3

To form the neck, connect the two shapes with two curved lines.

4

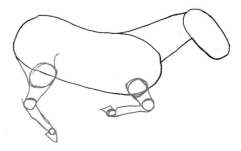

Then, draw three circles for the front leg and three more for the back leg. Draw lines to connect them as shown. Add the hooves.

5

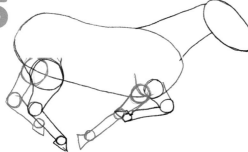

Now, form the other legs by drawing circles and connecting them with lines. Draw the hooves.

6

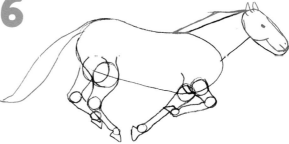

Add detail to the head by drawing the lower jaw, an eye, one nostril, the mouth, and both ears. Draw the shapes for the tail and mane as shown.

7

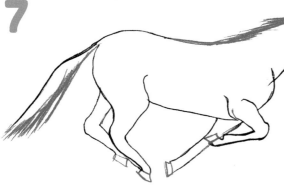

You can erase any extra lines. Then, hold the pencil with your index finger as you shade in the tail and the mane. Use the side of the pencil point at a slant, and make big, wide strokes. Your quarter horse is finished!

MEET THE APPALOOSA

Some horse breeds are hard to tell apart by color. However, the Appaloosa is easily identified by its color. That's because its coat has many spots and splashes of color. This type of horse is good at jumping and racing over both short and long distances.

The Appaloosa gets its name from the Palouse River, which flows in northwestern Idaho and southeastern Washington. It is believed that the breed was developed by a group of Native Americans called the Nez Percé who lived in that area. They rode Appaloosas into battle against the U.S. Cavalry. In 1975, the governor of Idaho signed a bill making the Appaloosa Idaho's state horse. Today, these horses are great for trail riding, racing, and working on ranches.

Appaloosas have different patterns on their coats. Some patterns are marble, leopard, snowflake, and blanket—a spotted blanket of white on the horse's hindquarters.

1

Begin by drawing an oval for the Appaloosa's body.

2

Next, draw a smaller oval for the head as shown. Notice where it's placed on the page compared to the first oval.

3

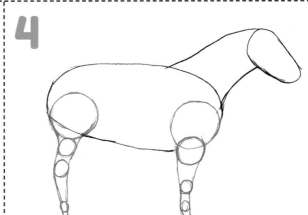

To draw the neck, connect the ovals with two curved lines.

4

Now, to make two of the legs, draw four circles for each leg. Connect the circles with two curved lines. Add the hooves.

5

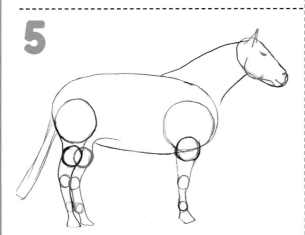

Follow the same steps as in Step 4 to form the other back leg. Draw circles, and then add two lines to join them. Draw in the lower jaw, an eye, the mouth, a nostril and ears.

6

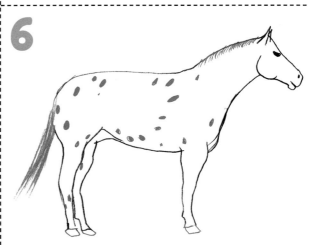

Erase the extra lines in the drawing. Now, you can add detail! Draw spots on your Appaloosa. Use the side of your pencil point at a slant to add the tail and mane.

MEET THE SHETLAND PONY

The Shetland pony is a small, strong horse. What's the difference between a horse and a pony? Its size! A pony is a type of horse that is smaller than most breeds. The Shetland pony is only 11 hands high, compared to 15 hands for the average horse breed. Although it's small, it's one of the strongest horses for its size.

Shetland ponies have thick coats and manes because they were raised on the Shetland Islands off the northern coast of Scotland, where it is often cold and rainy. The Shetland pony's combination of size and strength made it very useful for working in coal mines during the 19th century. Shetland ponies' thick fur keeps them warm in cold climates.

Shetlands are smart and sometimes a little stubborn. They are often used for horse rides for kids.

1

Begin by drawing an oval for the Shetland pony's body.

2

Now, draw a smaller oval for the head. Look to the illustration to see how it's placed above and to the right of the first oval.

3

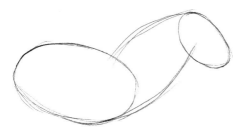

To make the neck, connect the ovals with two curved lines.

4

Add two of the legs by first drawing three circles for each leg. Draw two sets of curved lines as shown to join the circles. Add the hooves.

5

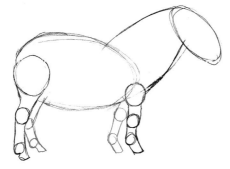

Now, follow the directions in Step 4 for the other legs. Draw the circles first, and then add the lines to join them. Add the other two hooves.

6

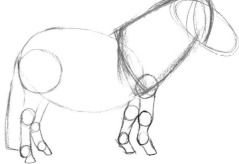

Look to the illustration as you draw the shapes of the tail and mane.

7

You can erase any extra lines. Add the small, curved line for the mouth. Shade in the tail and the mane by holding your pencil on its side at a slant. Make big, wide strokes. You've drawn a special Shetland pony!

MEET THE THOROUGHBRED

The word "thoroughbred" is often used to mean any purebred or **pedigree** horse. However, Thoroughbred is also a specific breed of horse. It is a crossbreed of several different types of horse breeds: Byerly Turk stallions, Dorley Arabian stallions, Gondolphin Barb stallions, and English mares.

The thoroughbred has a graceful head and neck, a long back and legs, and a broad chest. Its high energy makes it an excellent racehorse, polo pony, hunter, and jumper. One of the most famous Thoroughbreds was named Secretariat. In 1973, he won the Triple Crown, which means he won three special races that year: the Kentucky Derby, the Preakness, and the Belmont Stakes. Thoroughbreds are known to be spirited, sensitive, and graceful.

Adult Thoroughbreds are usually around 16 hands tall. They weigh about 1,000 pounds (453.4 kg).

**1**  Begin by drawing an oval for the Thoroughbred's body, tilted as shown.

2  Next, draw a smaller oval for the head tilted the opposite way from the big oval.

3 Draw two curved lines to connect the oval to make the neck.

4  Add four circles for each leg as shown to make the first two legs. Add two lines to connect the circles. Add the hooves.

5  Follow the same directions as Step 4 to draw the other legs.

6  Then, add some detail to the head by drawing the jaws, an eye, a nostril, the mouth, and both ears. Look to the illustration as you draw the shapes for the tail and mane.

7  Now, you can erase any extra lines. Fill in the tail and the mane by holding your pencil tip on its side. Make big, wide strokes. You've drawn your very own Thoroughbred champion!

GLOSSARY

adapt: To change to suit a situation or purpose.

agile: Able to move quickly yet easily and gracefully.

breed: A group of animals that look very much alike and have the same kind of relatives.

colonist: A person who lives in a colony, a place where they are still ruled by the leaders and laws of their old country.

conservation: Efforts to care for the natural world.

crossbreed: To cross two or more breeds within the same species to make babies.

develop: To grow.

domesticated: Tamed by humans.

nomadic: Traveling from place to place rather than settling down in one area.

pedigree: Referring to an impressive family history.

stagecoach: A horse-drawn carriage that carried passengers and mail to certain stops on a regular schedule.

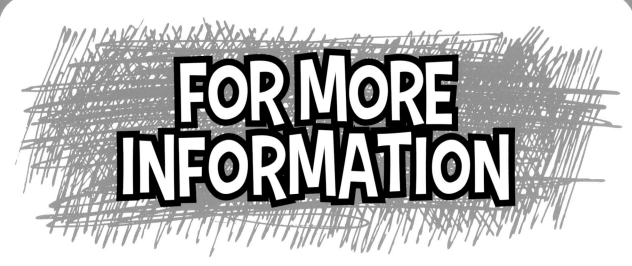
FOR MORE INFORMATION

WEBSITES

Horse

www.ducksters.com/animals/horse.php
Explore new horse facts, such as their diet and different coat colors.

Przewalski's Horse

kids.nationalgeographic.com/animals/mammals/facts/przewalskis-horse
Learn more about the Przewalski's horse when you visit this website.

BOOKS

DK. *The Everything Book of Horses and Ponies*. London, UK: DK Publishing, 2019.

Halls, Kelly Milner. *All About Horses: A Kid's Guide to Breeds, Care, Riding, and More!* Emeryville, CA: Rockridge Press, 2021.

INDEX